INTERCHANGE

Ken Jaworowski

I0139931

BROADWAY PLAY PUBLISHING INC
New York
www.broadwayplaypublishing.com
info@broadwayplaypublishing.com

INTERCHANGE

First printing: March 2015
I S B N: 978-0-88145-628-8

Book design: Marie Donovan
Page make-up: Adobe Indesign
Typeface: Palatino
Printed and bound in the U S A

ABOUT THE AUTHOR

Ken Jaworowski is a staff editor for *The New York Times*. His plays NEVER MISSED A DAY, CERTAIN SOULS and ACTS OF REDEMPTION have been performed in New York, London and elsewhere. His fiction and nonfiction appear in many publications.

INTERCHANGE was first performed at the WorkShop Theater in New York from 7-30 October 2010 The cast and creative contributors were:

DON	Gerry Goodstein
FRANK	Daniel Damiano
PROFESSOR UNSWORTH	Jeff Paul
VICTOR	David M Pincus
JOB REP/WOMAN/MARCIE	Shaun Bennet Wilson
LETTY	Cecily Benjamin
MARIE	Wende O'Reilly
MS JANSON	Riley Jones-Cohen
SIMON	Sean Singer
PROFESSOR BELLEVILLE	Liz Amberly
Director	Thomas Coté

CHARACTERS

DON, *a businessman in the old-school style.*
FRANK, *his son. A more flexible personality.*
PROFESSOR UNSWORTH, *a finance professor.*
VICTOR, *once a stockbroker, now a convicted felon recently
released from prison.*
JOB REP, *a worker in a temp agency*.*
LETTY, *a businesswoman.*
MARIE, *her boss.*
MS JANSON, *a case evaluator for a drug-treatment program.*
SIMON, *undergoing counseling for alcohol abuse.*
PROFESSOR BELLEVILLE, *a literature professor.*
WOMAN/MAN, *someone with an edge*.*
MARCIE, VICTOR's *ex-wife*.*

**These three parts were played by the same actress in the
premiere production.*

Scene 1

(Two men—a father, DON, about 55, and his son, FRANK, about 26—sit on beach chairs, holding fishing rods. DON is gruff, with no humor in his voice, even when telling a joke. FRANK is initially elusive. They look out at the water as they speak, not at each other.)

FRANK: Good day for it.

DON: It's not about the weather. It's about the tides. Strong tides.

FRANK: I hope the fish understand that.

DON: Fish're smart. Know why?

FRANK: They travel in schools.

DON: Yup.

FRANK: Ever think of getting a new joke?

DON: I stick with what works.

FRANK: That hasn't worked in years.

DON: *(Cheerlessly)* Not for you, maybe. Me, I'm laughin'. Internally. *(Pause. He cranes his neck, looks at someone further back on the beach.)*

FRANK: Who's that?

DON: Just somebody from the company.

FRANK: Not going to say hi?

DON: No.

FRANK: Don't be afraid to be friendly, Pop.

DON: I want a friend, I'll buy a dog.

FRANK: Ever think of taking an interest in people?

DON: More I meet people, more I like fish.

FRANK: I'm serious.

DON: So am I. Pipe down.

(Pause)

FRANK: You know how good I am at putting the worm on the hook?

(FRANK looks to DON but gets no response.)

FRANK: So good they call me the "master-baiter".

(DON, expressionless, stares at the ocean.)

FRANK: I bet you're laughin' internally.

(Pause as DON and FRANK look out at the water, taking in the silence. FRANK turns more serious.)

FRANK: You should...be nicer to people, Pop.

DON: *(Not pleased)* That what I should do?

FRANK: Yeah. I think...

DON: Don't go telling me what you think, O K? I've done well enough the way I am.

FRANK: Can you listen...?

DON: Being "nice" doesn't buy food. Didn't send you to school, or pay your bills, best doctors when you needed them. So don't go telling me about...

FRANK: I'm sorry. I don't want to fight. The last thing I want to do is fight.

DON: Then don't fight.

(Pause)

FRANK: I know it's not easy for you. I'm not perfect either. I'm just saying, maybe...try to be more patient. You always go for the throat...

DON: *(He's had enough. Over "throat")* Look, next time, don't call me when I got work to do, ask me to come out here if you're gonna give me a lecture. You got something to say, spit it out. If not, shut the hell up.

(Pause. Then quieter)

FRANK: It's a good spot to fish.

DON: Yeah.

FRANK: I hope I'm here next year to see it.

DON: What's that mean?

FRANK: The remission, it's…not…anymore. The doctor, he thinks this time isn't the same.

DON: What do you think?

FRANK: I don't feel so good, Pop. I think… If something…you might need to look after Danny.

DON: Tell me this ain't happening.

FRANK: I wish. But I can't. Test came back Wednesday. C'mon, we knew this could happen since I was sixteen…I'm…sorry.

DON: My god, don't apologize.

FRANK: Your age, shouldn't be stuck with a seven-year-old. But no mother, now this.

DON: *(Still bewildered)* Why'd you let me yell at you?

FRANK: I been trying to make you stop since I was a kid.

DON: I didn't…I don't mean it. It's just who I am.

FRANK: I know. I haven't told Danny. You and I…It's been tough. But him, he's not so strong yet. You gotta be good to him, O K? I need you to be…different. Show him you can be kind. Just do that.

DON: I will. I wish…I'd trade with you right now if I could…

FRANK: I know you would.

(FRANK *tentatively touches* DON's *shoulder? Or stops himself just before?* DON *continues to look out at the water.*)

FRANK: *(Softly)* So…think we're gonna catch anything?

DON: *(Very far away)* I hope so, my son. God, I hope so.

(End of scene)

Scene 2

(PROFESSOR UNSWORTH *enters a classroom, carrying a briefcase, and stands at a lectern or desk. He opens the briefcase, takes out a thick textbook and places it on top. He is smartly dressed, but not fashionably. He's been lecturing for years and is soft-spoken and constant in his methods. He has a tic about the book—perhaps he occasionally runs his hand over the cover, or unthinkingly picks it up and puts it down. He addresses the audience as his class.*)

PROFESSOR: Good morning. Please turn to Page 146. We'll go over the text as Mister Carver lowers the lights for the overhead. You'll read that, ah…
(On "you'll", he looks up from the book to see that some of the class is already drifting off. He realizes their disinterest.)
Um…Mister Carver…just a moment. Before we begin…
Close your books, please.
Thank you for filling out the midterm professor evaluations.
The department passes on your anonymous comments. To quote one student: 'I'm a Buddhist. As Professor Unsworth lectures I wonder what I did in a past life to deserve the suffering.' And from another scholar: 'I can sum up the class in two words: Not. Much. Fun.'
(Beat. He is hurt by the remarks though tries not to show it)

I'm sorry the class is "not much fun". But Financial Analysis and Decision Strategies is…

The concepts are challenging. Still, it's important and…

But I can't ignore the obvious. You aren't comfortable with the material. So let's try a different tack.

I was speaking with Professor Belleville, of the English department.

She suggested using examples to help with the abstract concepts.

So to illustrate today's topic: a story.

It's from the novel *A Lonelier Time*. The scene takes place in the dustbowl, in the 1930s. Banks foreclosed on thousands of properties. People starved to death in the winters.

There was a poor family, five of them: a young man, his wife and their child, and his aged father and mother. They owned a small plot of land. Together they worked, put everything into the wheat crop. Hoping that after the harvest, they could sell it and pay their debts before their home was seized.

One morning, when the wheat was ready for harvest, a panic spread through the nearby town: A swarm of locusts was approaching. The crops would be destroyed. Unless they hurried. They raced to the field to save what they could.

In their rush, a sickle fell from a cart, cutting the old father very badly.

The question then became: Do you run to town, try to find a doctor to save your father, but then lose your home and starve over the winter? Or do you watch him die as you save everything you have? Your decision must be made immediately.

(Beat as he waits for them to contemplate.)

This is not what you call a…a "feel gooder".

But these are the choices you may face in the real world. A financial aspect is there, even when it doesn't appear so.
(Beat. He reaches for the book)
With that in mind, turn to Page 146. Mister Carver, bring down the lights for the overhead. I'll...
Hmmm?
Professor Belleville was right! She said someone would ask for the ending. She said my answer should be: "Go read the book".
(A smile. Pleased with himself)
That was fun, wasn't it?
So...
(He wants to go on with the example, almost considers it, then remembers his obligation to the material. His voice takes on a more serious, dull tone.)
On Page 146, when the yield curve flattens. This is exciting. When the yield curve flattens, what happens? Uh...anyone? Anyone...
Would anyone like...to...guess? *(Half a smile, but terribly disappointed)* Anyone?
(Beat)
Mister Carver, could you, uh, could you...bring down the lights?

(The lights come down.)

(End of scene)

Scene 3

(VICTOR walks into a spare room with a single desk. He wears a shirt and tie that have become wrinkled after a day of walking. He hands a sheet of paper to a REP who sits behind the desk. She looks at it, pauses for a moment over a section, then finishes the examination and places the paper in a basket of other forms.)

VICTOR: I'm sorry. I don't have a resume yet. But I think I filled this out right.

REP: We'll call if something's available.

VICTOR: I can start tomorrow. Heck, I can start right now.

(*The* REP *nods, tries to get back to work, expecting* VICTOR *to leave.*)

VICTOR: Last couple people, seems like you had something for them. Any chance…?

(*The* REP *gives him a look, glances down at* VICTOR's *application, and perhaps a motion that says "Probably not, but who knows".*)

VICTOR: Because of…?

REP: It's the first thing they look at. They tell us, no criminal records. You might try someplace else.

VICTOR: I've been to every temp agency. I got out three weeks ago. If I don't find something, they'll send me back.

REP: Sorry.

VICTOR: I've got a degree in accounting. Top Ten school. Good experience too.

REP: Why were you in jail?

VICTOR: I was a broker. Got a line on a fund that would take off. Moved accounts without them knowing— everyone would win. Stupid. It was…out of character. Then the guy: his fund was a fraud. Everyone lost everything. (*Beat*) I'm saying, there was no malice. I lost it all too.

REP: See, it varies by company. But generally they don't like employees who steal. They hate the competition.

VICTOR: Yeah. Well. I gotta be a hundred percent honest…I'm at the end of my rope. I've been walking around twelve hours a day. Nothing.
I have a son…he was born when I was in jail. I've never seen him. When I get on my feet, I will. I don't care what the job is. I used to work twelve-hour days. I was so proud of that. *(Beat)* Anything at all. Please.

(A longer pause. The REP *and* VICTOR *both look at each other.)*

VICTOR: You know, if this was a movie, this is where you'd give me a chance.

REP: If this was a movie, I'd be in Aruba, not talkin' to you.

VICTOR: Yeah.

REP: *(She sighs, digs out a card.)* Do you like animals? Cats, dogs…?

VICTOR: You want the truth?

REP: No.

VICTOR: Then I love 'em.

REP: There's a kennel. For pets. To board them.

VICTOR: What will I do? Bookkeeping or…or billing? I can do that.

REP: No. Cleaning cages. Wiping them out.

VICTOR: Oh. That's the only…?

REP: Really, that's all I have for you.

VICTOR: A'right.

REP: You'd have to sign as an independent contractor. No benefits.

VICTOR: I'll do it.

REP: The hours are bad.

VICTOR: 'k.

REP: The pay is terrible.

VICTOR: You're doing a fine job of selling it.

(The REP *looks at* VICTOR *with a warning. Perhaps she starts to put the card away.)*

VICTOR: I'll take it.

REP: Come back Friday with two forms of I D.

VICTOR: Alright. *(He turns to leave.)*

REP: Wait wait wait. *(Finds a form)* You need a bond before you can work.

VICTOR: What kind of…?

REP: Independent means you buy your own insurance, against theft, or…

VICTOR: I won't steal a poodle or…

REP: Or if you break something. It's required. I'd make my own granny get one. *(Hands him the form)* Go here, get the bond, they'll send me the certificate.

VICTOR: How much does that cost?

REP: The price is at the bottom.

VICTOR: You're kidding. I don't have that.

(The REP *holds out her hand for the form.* VICTOR *instead puts it in his pocket.)*

REP: First thing, Friday morning. So you need to get the bond before then.

VICTOR: O K. You'd make your own grandmother get one?

REP: Especially her. She's a wingnut.

VICTOR: Alright.

REP: And if you don't get the bond…I can't help you.

(Lights down.)

(End of scene)

Scene 4

(LETTY *half knocks and sticks her head in* MARIE's *office.*
LETTY *is outgoing but she's been on the wrong end of*
MARIE's *temper and knows to use caution.* MARIE *is sitting,*
looking down at some papers. Both are in business dress.)

LETTY: Hey. I was going to let Mike and Kate leave.

MARIE: It's not five yet.

LETTY: There's nothing left for them to do.

MARIE: *(Looks up from her papers. Flatly)* You're serious.

LETTY: It's only fifteen minutes. I just thought...

MARIE: Yeah, and that's called 'time theft.' You *keep*
them here, even if there's nothing.

LETTY: Of course.

MARIE: Come. Sit.

(LETTY enters and sits.)

MARIE: You've been here a year now?

LETTY: Yes.

MARIE: And still, once a week I find myself...

LETTY: I'm sorry. I...

MARIE: I'm speaking. This isn't a playground. We're in
a shit economy. In a ruthless industry. Last week I laid
off three people. You think that was fun?

LETTY: No.

MARIE: I mean, it was a *little* fun, because I hated them.
But then I had to put up with their crying. Remember
when we had the opening in this group? You said you
could handle pressure. That you were tough. We're
management. They need to understand that.

LETTY: O K.

MARIE: The way you can pick apart a contract—it's great work. Even better—there's something in your eyes that says you could be a fighter. I want us to cultivate that.

LETTY: I'll work on it.

MARIE: Now. The R B A conference.

LETTY: With the legal seminars…?

MARIE: Exactly. *Bullshit*. But a certified rep needs to be there or we lose accreditation. Everyone hates it. Guess who goes this year?

LETTY: Spence?

MARIE: No. You. You'll love it.

LETTY: This is…

MARIE: Book a flight and hotel. It's only a week. You'll survive.

LETTY: I…

MARIE: What?

LETTY: There's… There's no one else who can go?

MARIE: That's why you're certified, as a backup. What's the matter now?

LETTY: I have to be honest about something. I'm pregnant.

MARIE: Hey! Congratulations! Wait, are you quitting?

LETTY: No. I can't leave. My husband's salary barely covers the rent.

MARIE: And when the baby…?

LETTY: My mom will be our nanny. But now, the doctor said I'm high risk. I can't get on a plane.

MARIE: How far along are you?

LETTY: Two months this week.

MARIE: *(She thinks about this a second.)* Wait. Two months ago…you were on sick leave. With pneumonia. *(Beat)* You weren't sick.

LETTY: I…ah…

MARIE: Tell me the truth.

LETTY: I went to a clinic in Grand Harbor for a procedure. I'm sorry. I'd already used up all my vacation trying. This was my last chance. I was scared. I had to make up a story.

MARIE: This is great.

LETTY: *(Smiles)* I know.

MARIE: Not that you're pregnant. That you could lie. *That's* what I'm looking for. So what about the conference?

LETTY: There must be someone else. Aren't…you certified?

MARIE: Am I certified? I was. But you need twenty hours of instruction to keep current. After this year, do you think I had time to re-up?

LETTY: No one else?

MARIE: Well, there's Spence. March in there and ask the C E O to go. Oh, and tell him you lied about sick leave. He's fired a dozen people for tricks like that.

LETTY: Isn't there anyone?

MARIE: Maybe Don, down at the Peermont office.

LETTY: Can I ask him?

MARIE: That prick. You'll never get him to do it.

LETTY: Can I try?

MARIE: Go right ahead. Let me know how it goes. It's your responsibility now. We can*not* lose accreditation. That's it.

(*As* LETTY *reaches the door:*)

MARIE: Maybe you should let Mike and Kate go.

LETTY: It's not five yet.

MARIE: That's better. Now you're learning.

(*End of scene*)

Scene 5

(*The office of* MS JANSON. SIMON *enters carrying a backpack. He's angry to be there, and barely keeps it under control.*)

JANSON: Have a seat. Hello.

(JANSON *gets no response.* SIMON *sits. A brief pause. She looks at a form.*)

JANSON: Mr. Castle. Or should I call you Simon?

(SIMON *doesn't answer.* JANSON *turns from friendly to tough with no effort.*)

JANSON: You're required to answer. If not, your file goes back to your probation officer. You'll fail substance-abuse counseling and off to county you go, for your six-month sentence. (*Beat*) So: Mister Castle, or Simon?

SIMON: Simon.

JANSON: Fine. I'm Ms Janson.

SIMON: Wait—then call me Mister Castle.

JANSON: Sorry, no switching. When was your last drink?

SIMON: Six days ago. I quit.

JANSON: Well, my job is done. *(Beat)* I hope you're not lying.

SIMON: I don't lie. I got some self-respect, O K?

JANSON: So it's respectable to wing a shot glass at a bartender's face?

SIMON: He said I owed him money. I counted. He was trying to rip me off.

JANSON: *(Rolls her eyes, hands him a paper)* Here. Your schedule. We meet twice a week to chart your progress. You have group counseling Tuesdays and Thursdays, starting this evening.

SIMON: Can I go now?

JANSON: Next time I want to know why you drink so much. And why you're so angry, Simon.

SIMON: I'm not angry. *(He opens his bag to stuff the schedule inside. He stands in a hurry and a gun and a pack of cigarettes falls out. Puts his foot over the gun in a weak attempt to hide it)*

JANSON: What is that?

SIMON: My cigarettes.

JANSON: What else?

SIMON: Lint.

JANSON: *(She picks up the phone)* I'm calling the police.

SIMON: It's a Colt nine millimeter.

JANSON: Why is it here?

SIMON: Long story.

JANSON: They pay me by the hour.

SIMON: *(Genuinely surprised)* Do they?

JANSON: *(Still dead serious)* No. But they should. Why do you have that?

SIMON: I have a permit! Isn't that in my file?

JANSON: But carrying a gun on probation? *(After a moment's thought she puts down the phone.)* I'm confiscating that and writing you up for...

SIMON: Please! It's an honest mistake! I'll lock it up at home. I'll never bring it again!

JANSON: Why do you have it at all?

SIMON: I got it in case of robbery. My dad and I, we had a little store, before he died.

JANSON: Was there a hold-up?

SIMON: No. We lost our money and the store went under. That's what killed him—heart attack, two days after we closed. All the stress.

JANSON: Do not bring that gun back.

SIMON: I won't. Ever.

JANSON: *(She takes some pamphlets and hands him one.)* Get it out of here. Go. And before next time, read this. It's about how to discuss your drinking problem. Give them to the people you're close to.

SIMON: I told you, I ain't got a family.

JANSON: Your friends then.

(Beat. SIMON is silent.)

JANSON: Who...who do you talk to about all this? *(Silence)* Who do you go out drinking with?

SIMON: Myself.

(Beat. SIMON's loneliness dawns on JANSON, though she tries to remain clinical.)

JANSON: Don't you have anyone to...?

SIMON: You know what it takes to run a store? I worked eighty hours a week!

JANSON: What do you do in your free time now?

SIMON: I…just been thinking a lot lately. Maybe that's my problem…I've never seen the store since we lost it. I was wondering…maybe I should. Take a look, ya know?

JANSON: Sure.

SIMON: *(A beat, then quieter, a little embarrassed, even boyish)* Do you wanna go?

JANSON: Where?

SIMON: To see the store. You said we gotta talk. We could, on the way. I could tell you about it. My dad and I had some good times there.

JANSON: Oh. My schedule, it's…

SIMON: I was gonna leave from here. See it in the daylight.

JANSON: I…there's…

(SIMON *looks at* JANSON. *An embarrassed pause)*

SIMON: Yeah, I know. You got people waiting.

JANSON: If I'd have known, I could…

SIMON: No. It was dumb. I shouldn't have asked… stupid…

JANSON: Wait a…

SIMON: You're already late for your clients. Don't keep the alkies waiting.

JANSON: We can talk next meeting, O K? Long as you want.

SIMON: *(He walks to the door in a huff)* Yeah.

JANSON: One last question: Why do you still carry a gun if you don't have the store?

SIMON: I have a permit.

JANSON: That's not an answer.

SIMON: Well, because I want to.

JANSON: Think you know it all, huh?

SIMON: That's another question. You're over your limit.

JANSON: I don't know why you're acting like this.
Underneath, you seem…only marginally an asshole.
(Beat, then more serious.) Be careful who you pretend to
be. You could turn into that person.

(End of scene)

Scene 6

*(PROFESSOR BELLEVILLE is in line in the cafeteria, holding
a tray. UNSWORTH approaches her nervously. He comes
up behind her, leans around her side and smiles widely and
genuinely. She sees him and smiles too.)*

*(Their dialogue is filled with pauses and stalls, more like
awkward schoolchildren with crushes. They are overly
apologetic and deathly afraid of making a mistake.)*

UNSWORTH: Ah, hey. Hello Professor Belleville.

BELLEVILLE: Oh, hi!

UNSWORTH: Thanks again for helping me find that
story.

BELLEVILLE: How did it go?

UNSWORTH: The class loved it. They were…what do
you call it…*awake!* This one kid who always sleeps,
drooling on his desk, he was… *(He makes a funny face, of
someone waking up, shocked and attentive, and drooling.)*

BELLEVILLE: *(Happily)* That's revolting!

UNSWORTH: *(Embarrassed)* Oh. Sorry. Stupid. Talking
about drool at lunch.

BELLEVILLE: No, I…I meant 'revolting' in the *good* way!
I didn't mean…

UNSWORTH: I didn't...Oh. Well, thank you. Again.

BELLEVILLE: My pleasure.

(BELLEVILLE *and* UNSWORTH *both smile, but those smiles fade a little bit as they wait in line, at a loss for words.*)

BELLEVILLE: Um...If you...need any more help, let me know.

UNSWORTH: I will. How was your class?

BELLEVILLE: Interesting. We're comparing Victorian women—how they flirted—with today. In contrast, we're reading *The Rules*—how modern women play "hard to get". How they act uninterested...but then how they hint where they'll be later so the guy will meet them.

UNSWORTH: Sounds fun.

BELLEVILLE: It provokes a lot of discussion.

UNSWORTH: How've things changed for men?

BELLEVILLE: For them it's always the same—show control, be confident.

UNSWORTH: Absolutely. Right. Right.

(UNSWORTH *points forward to show there's free space in line, or picks up something with authority.* BELLEVILLE *and* UNSWORTH *step up a space, he with a military bearing.*)

BELLEVILLE: But women also want someone agreeable.

UNSWORTH: Oh, of course there do! Of course. That's true.

BELLEVILLE: It depends on the situation. Sometimes you show interest, sometimes you play hard to get.

UNSWORTH: Would you like to sit together?

BELLEVILLE: I'd love to! But...I, uh, may be...busy...

UNSWORTH: Oh.

BELLEVILLE: Oh.

(BELLEVILLE *and* UNSWORTH *both pause again, paralyzed with nervousness. Finally* UNSWORTH *looks out over the cafeteria.*)

UNSWORTH: I think…

BELLEVILLE: *(Turns around, happily)* Yes?

UNSWORTH: Someone's waving to you.

BELLEVILLE: Oh. The dean of the "Anguish" department. I was hoping he wouldn't see me. We're supposed to meet over lunch.

UNSWORTH: Oh. O K.

BELLEVILLE: But after that, I guess I'll just go to the library, between two and three o'clock. I have work there on the first floor. Near the back. Is where I usually am.

UNSWORTH: Oh. That's when I have my class.

BELLEVILLE: *(Still trying to act uninterested)* I usually stay until three or four.

UNSWORTH: Then maybe I'll see you. When I have no class.

(BELLEVILLE *laughs.*)

UNSWORTH: *(Embarrassed, thinking he's an idiot)* I didn't mean I don't have class. I mean, when I'm out of…

BELLEVILLE: *(Horrified she laughed)* I didn't mean to laugh. I'm sorry. I…I thought you were joking.

UNSWORTH: No, I wasn't.

BELLEVILLE: Oh. Heh.

UNSWORTH: Yeah. Heh.

(BELLEVILLE *and* UNSWORTH *both sort of turn away from each other, embarrassed, rolling their eyes at their own perceived stupidity.*)

(End of scene)

Scene 7

(DON's office after 5 P M. LETTY arrives. They shake hands.)

DON: Letty. How are ya?

LETTY: Good. Thanks for staying late to meet me.

DON: Not a problem. Coffee?

LETTY: No. But thank you.

DON: How's things back at the big leagues?

LETTY: Fine. How's business here?

DON: Lots of walk-ins, small policies and stuff.

LETTY: *(Carefully)* Good. Don, I was so sorry to hear, about your son. You got my card and flowers?

DON: Yes. That was kind. Thank you. Well, let me get you something. I'll make tea.

LETTY: Nothing for me.

DON: We can send out for dinner. My treat.

LETTY: You've always been *straight* to business. Now you're asking to make me tea. It's almost...cute. This a new idea from a business book?

DON: Ah, it's nothing. I'm trying to be more...open. I'd rather not talk about it.

LETTY: Oh. O K.

DON: So what can I do for ya? Or you just here to get away from that wolverine you work for?

LETTY: Oh, she's not so bad.

DON: Right. I shouldn't be mean. So how's...your boss?

LETTY: Fine.

DON: I'm...happy to hear that. What's she want?

LETTY: It's about the R B A conference. I...we need you to go.

DON: Me? Nah, I can't go to a conference.

LETTY: Oh, come on, Don. It'll be fun to go, hang out with the...

DON: No. I have to make that clear, right off the bat. Anything else you want, it's yours. Just not that.

LETTY: Don. It's important for the company.

DON: Who else is certified? Are you?

LETTY: Yes, but I can't go. Why can't you?

DON: *(He doesn't want to get personal, but can't avoid telling.)* My grandson. It's me and him now. My son and his girlfriend, they were kids themselves when they had him. She skipped out. I'm all alone too... He's shaken up after his father...you know...I can't leave him.

LETTY: Oh. Is there any way...Maybe you could bring him with you?

DON: You know, I...I'm trying not to be the damn... jerk I was. But if you'd asked me that question last year, I... *(Curls his fist, by his side. His anger subsides a bit.)* Nah, I'd have gone. But now...I'm not bringing this kid to a conference, or leaving him with some stranger. You're at headquarters, it's your job to go.

LETTY: Marie gave me full authority to...I...I don't want to use that authority.

DON: Then don't.

LETTY: But you...

DON: But nothin'. Have a heart, will ya? You don't have to have kids to understand how...

LETTY: Whoa, Don. Now don't... You have to go.

(Beat. DON motions for LETTY to sit. She does so reluctantly. The unfamiliarity of speaking like he is about to is difficult. He starts, quietly, even pleasantly.)

DON: I'm from the old school. Sometimes, I look
around, I don't know what the hell happened.
Handshake for a deal, pay in cash, that's how I started.
But I want to talk to you, personal, for a minute...

LETTY: Don...

DON: Please. I made this promise. You see, my
son...He was sick, a long time. His cancer went into
remission twice before, so you think it's all gonna
blow over. But when it came back the last time...he got
so weak.*(Beat)* My Frank, wasted away in a hospital
bed. We're strugglin' to talk about good times we
had. It was...embarrassing, 'cause we never did much
together. I...I thought I was being a decent father, you
know? *(Beat, then bitterly)* No. I was too concerned
about money. See, that's how my father raised my
brother and me, to keep working. To be strong. *(Beat)*
And I'm sitting there with my boy. And I ain't never
said it to him before. But I knew I had to, else I'd never
get the chance. I said to him: "I love you, my son". It
took all I had but I said it and I *meant* it. *(Beat)* He said:
"I appreciate that, dad". *(Beat)* But ya see...he never...
And me, guy who's a legend around here 'cause he
ain't afraid of nothin', I'm scared to ask my own son,
whether... I'm *sittin'* there, hintin' around, hoping and
hoping that he...

LETTY: Don, there's nothing I can...

DON: *You listen to me now!* My *son!* On his *deathbed!*
Would not tell me he loved me! And I sat there like
some fool, hoping my boy would tell me but he *didn't!*
Hell, why should he? Who was I? Some stranger who
worked all the time, then bitched at him when I paid
the bills. *(Beat)* At night...he faded. And I sat there
knowing he wasn't gonna wake up...and realizing
the way I lived my life had been all wrong. *(Beat. He
grows cold as his anger subsides.)* Well. He wouldn't say

it, but at least he was honest: I taught him never to lie to his father. *(Beat. He's coming back to normal.)* Now I promised to be a man his son could be proud of. So don't you come in here and ask me to break my word to my boy. After all I done for this company, I won't have it.

LETTY: *(She's getting upset. Perhaps touches her stomach. Then, more to herself:)* I have…I have to go.

DON: I tell you something I never told anybody, you tell me you gotta go?

LETTY: *(Gathers her things)* I'm sorry, Don. I'll send you your reservations.

DON: Unbelievable. You pulling this "company above all" when a couple months back, I hear you're in bed with pneumonia, then I see you walkin' the beach.

LETTY: I…

DON: My son and I were in Grand Harbor, fishing. I saw you there. If I hadn't just promised him not to be a hard-ass, I'd have called up Spence, you'd be fired on the spot. Lying like that when this company is talking about more job cuts.

LETTY: There…there's this clinic. You don't understand…

DON: I don't care. I'm just telling you, I'm not going to a conference. I'm through with all that.

LETTY: I'm not going either, Don.

DON: We're in a standoff then, huh?

(Both DON and LETTY stare at each other, holding their ground.)

DON: Who you think's gonna win?

(End of scene)

Scene 8

(VICTOR *sits on a high stool in a room, a bright light on him.*
He's shamed and quiet in his embarrassment. He speaks
throughout almost as if to himself. A WOMAN *stands a*
few feet away, dressed with an edge. Their talk is clipped, a
result of his nervousness. She moves around mostly in the
darkness.)

WOMAN: So I'm curious: Who sent you to me?

VICTOR: I was outside a temp agency. Some guy said
if I needed money...I need it by tomorrow and I can't
find anything. He said come here.

WOMAN: Oh sure, sure. I was only wondering.

VICTOR: I looked everywhere.

WOMAN: You don't have to make excuses. I'm sure it's
difficult.

VICTOR: Can we just...?

WOMAN: Absolutely. Make yourself comfortable.

VICTOR: I don't want to be comfortable. I don't want to
be here at all. I want to get some money and go.

WOMAN: Oh, I totally understand. Totally.

VICTOR: I don't do this. This one time and then I can get
a real job. I just want to work.

WOMAN: Of course.

VICTOR: So the money is in cash?

WOMAN: Yes. You know the rate. Unless you'd like to
earn extra.

VICTOR: No. *(Holds out his hand)*

WOMAN: I'm really sorry, but I make payment
afterwards.

VICTOR: O K.

WOMAN: Stand there, please.

VICTOR: Do I need to…

WOMAN: No. Not yet.

VICTOR: O K.

WOMAN: Did your friend tell you I only work with former inmates?

VICTOR: He's not my friend. He said…

WOMAN: Only real people. Authentic. There's a nice market.

VICTOR: Look, I don't care about this.

WOMAN: I got another guy coming in, if you two want to…

VICTOR: No.

(WOMAN *steps back and takes a cover off a camera that rest on a tripod. She turns it on, and the light hurts* VICTOR's *eyes.*)

WOMAN: Because the people who like these pay a lot more.

VICTOR: No. You said it was me and no one else.

WOMAN: Of course. No offense. And you recently got out?

VICTOR: Yeah.

WOMAN: When?

VICTOR: Three weeks ago.

WOMAN: Speak up please.

VICTOR: Three weeks ago. Is there…?

WOMAN: Yes. Audio. For the Web site. They like my voice in the background.

VICTOR: I didn't know this was for…

WOMAN: It's not just pictures. *(Beat)* Those two guys you met coming in? They can escort you out.

VICTOR: Just. Go ahead.

WOMAN: So you've been out of jail for how long?

VICTOR: *(Quietly, as if to himself)* Three weeks.

WOMAN: Speak up.

VICTOR: Three weeks.

WOMAN: Did you like it in there?

VICTOR: What do you think?

WOMAN: Oh, that's tough, isn't it. *(She waits and gets no response. A bit more of an angry edge surfaces)* I said, isn't it? *(She still gets no response.)* Take off your shirt.

(VICTOR begins to unbutton)

WOMAN: Slower. Did you like being behind bars?

VICTOR: *(Barely audible)* No.

WOMAN: What did you say? Tell the camera.
Do you want your money? You came here. Asked me to do you a favor, didn't you? *(No response)* Getting angry? Huh, big man? *(Her voice has now revealed himself as malicious, even hateful.)* Well, if you want your money, you'll listen to *me*. Look in the camera. You want the money, I can tell. Now take your fucking clothes the fuck off…

(The camera light is now almost blindingly bright on VICTOR before blackout.)

(End of scene)

Scene 9

(SIMON *enters* JANSON'*s office.*)

JANSON: Hello again.

SIMON: Hello.

JANSON: No gun?

SIMON: No.

JANSON: So how are you?

SIMON: I don't feel like talking.

(Pause. JANSON *sits there, unfazed and unafraid to be quiet.)*

SIMON: I got nothing to say. *(Looks around the room. Pause.)* I don't need to talk to anyone anyway. *(Tries to stop. Can't)* So I ain't saying anything. To you at least. *(Pause. He can't help himself.)* People like you. Always so confident. You're the kind who screw up this world. Like the guy who killed my dad.

JANSON: I thought it wasn't a hold-up?

SIMON: Same thing! We had all our money with this one guy. He promised us it was safe. Yeah, right. Guess who lost everything? Us. You can kill someone in a million ways. That's what that guy needs to learn.

JANSON: What does that mean?

SIMON: If a guy killed someone in your family, what would you do to him?

JANSON: Is this why you were drinking? Because you wanted to kill someone?

SIMON: I was drinking so I *wouldn't* kill someone. That guy just got out of jail. I found his address. So I'd get drunk. That stops me from going over there. I don't want to drink and drive. I could hurt somebody.

JANSON: Well that's good.

SIMON: Why do you care? You get paid no matter what happens to me.

JANSON: You think this is about money? If I wanted real money I'd be a stripper.

(JANSON *gets* VICTOR *to grin.*)

JANSON: Is that a smile? I care because you might get hurt. You're *young.* That means you're *dumb.* And it's my professional opinion that you have problems. Since I'm only your case evaluator, I'm going to recommend you see a psychologist or…

SIMON: Aw, not another meeting! That group therapy is like Dawn of the Dead! All whiners and complainers and no one with the guts to take any action…

JANSON: Do you have a church? A priest or a counselor or…

SIMON: I got a priest, yeah. But he's as old as a fossil.

JANSON: Start there. You need to discuss this with someone qualified. Have him contact me. Otherwise I'll require you to see…

SIMON: Do whatever you want.

JANSON: Why is everything so angry?

SIMON: What's wrong with being angry?

JANSON: Nothing. Unless it overtakes your life.

SIMON: Don't worry about my life.

JANSON: I can't help but care. A little. (*Beat, then trying to be lighthearted.*) The rest is just for the money.

SIMON: Well, pretend. Pretend you don't care. See how that works for you. (*Gets up and goes, angrily.*)

(*End of scene*)

Scene 10

(LETTY *and* MARIE *on an elevator.*)

LETTY: I didn't have a choice. He knew I lied about sick leave. I had to tell him I was pregnant.

MARIE: So who's going to the conference?

LETTY: He thinks he might work something out.

MARIE: You said he screamed at you!

LETTY: He did. But after I told him about the baby, we sat and talked for a while.

MARIE: Oh, he's suckered you in! Think about it: He has all this information on you, then he says he needs time to work something out.

LETTY: He's not going to call Spence.

MARIE: He's always been a prick, but says he's changed. And you're betting everything on that? Your job? Your baby?

LETTY: He won't…

MARIE: Right. And now you're folding.

LETTY: Marie…the man lost his son a couple months ago.

MARIE: *(Goes quieter, colder)* I overheard you once, telling Nancy you were afraid of turning into a bitch. I assume you were talking about me.

LETTY: No, I…!

MARIE: Well, here's a real bitch: If someone doesn't go to that conference, we lose accreditation. Without that, a sixth of our revenue: gone. I walk in the next day, five people get fired. Think Nancy will like the unemployment line? Carl, with his two kids? *You?* That is *reality*. You're worried about *Don?* A retail office in Bumfuck used to be impossible to staff. Today I can find a dozen who'll take that job.

LETTY: If you were me, what would you...?

MARIE: If I were you, I wouldn't *be* in this situation. I'd care about myself before I got screwed over. But this is your problem. Find us a solution. I'd be open to anything. Have a nice night.

(Elevator opens. MARIE *steps off first and leaves.)*

(End of scene)

Scene 11

*(*DON *is alone at home. He dials the phone, gets nervous, hangs up. The same thing again. Finally he steels himself and makes the call. He waits, gets a machine.)*

DON: Hey. It's me. Those hang-ups on your machine... uh...the phone slipped out of my hand. A lot of times.

After Frank's funeral, it got me thinking. You're my only brother. Maybe we should. You know. I dunno...

I meant what I said at the funeral. You look good. It's been years since I saw you.

You made little Danny smile. He's been yapping away about his uncle. You made him happy.

That's what it's all about, huh? Being happy?

I called about a problem I'm having at work. I'm sitting here and I realize...

I ain't got no one else to talk to. Ain't that funny? At my age.

Heh. But you're family. You're required to listen, huh? *(Beat)* Plus, I know where you live.

Frank, he made me promise to be a better person. And I don't mind sayin': This nice-guy shit ain't easy.

This work problem…I might need your help.

I'll say this on your machine since I might chicken out in person, but…let's forget the past.

Be friends, O.K.?

(Beat. Quieter)

When we were kids, with dad, we thought the world would get easier, huh?

(He has nothing else to say. He begins to put the phone down. As the phone is almost on the cradle he realizes he hasn't said goodbye and pulls the phone back.)

I hope…you call me.

(End of scene)

Scene 12

(A church. Perhaps a cross projected on the wall. SIMON enters a confessional, kneels, looks into the small window.)

SIMON: Bless me Father for…I'm thinking of sinning. It's been like ten years since my last confession. The last time was with you, Father. You've been here forever, huh? In school we joked that you once met Jesus. When you were middle-aged.
I can't buy it, that there's a God who cares for us. My dad, worked his whole life, then someone took it all away. Why would God do something like that? Humiliate him?
I can't get it out of my head, that the guy who did it should be punished. I feel that in my heart, so deep. I hate him.
And I sit there at night, wondering why we're even alive. To make money? To love each other? But what's love worth when it's gone and you got nobody?

This guy. I'm gonna go to him. I'm not sure what to
do. But if hate's a sin, I should say every prayer in the
book.

I'm sorry Father. I don't know why I came. Thought I'd
try to talk it out. Maybe it helps a little. So forgive me if
you can, before I commit the sin.

(Hoping the priest will talk him out of it:)

I'm leaving now, Father, O K? Do *not* try to talk me out
of this, alright? 'Cause...'cause I won't listen. Got it?
Don't even *try*.

*(No response. He stands, opens the curtain and looks into
the priest's chamber.)*

*(Almost as if talking to a child. Very kindly, and full of care
for the old man, though he's deeply sad he still hasn't found
someone to talk to.)*

Wake up, Father. No, I'm not making a confession, I
just...How you feeling? *(Beat. Tries to smile)* Ninety-
two, huh? Well you sure look good. I stopped in to say
'hi,' that's all. Take care, Father. Take care.

(End of scene)

Scene 13

*(MARCIE, early 30s, enters a park, sees VICTOR waiting on
a bench for her. He rises. She's cold, though underneath she
can't help but care for him a little. He is near the end of his
rope, ashamed to be there, but holding it together.)*

VICTOR: Hello.

MARCIE: Hello.

VICTOR: Thank you for meeting me.

MARCIE: You're welcome.

VICTOR: I've been out three weeks now.

MARCIE: O K.

VICTOR: I'm doing well, thank you for asking.

MARCIE: If you're going to fight, I'll leave.

VICTOR: I don't want to fight.

MARCIE: What do you want?

VICTOR: I wanted to give you my address. I'm staying at my mother's old place.

MARCIE: It's been condemned.

VICTOR: What else do I have? I'm burning candles in there. But after I get on my feet, I'll buy you dinner. We'll have a lot to…

MARCIE: You can't call me again.

VICTOR: I have to.

MARCIE: I'm living with someone.

VICTOR: I'm…not surprised. I figured you'd…

MARCIE: We're getting married.

VICTOR: *(A little stung)* Congratulations, I guess. Who is it?

MARCIE: Steve. Steve Lennox.

VICTOR: From down the block? That…dick? No offense Marcie, he's the biggest tool I ever met. This is the first time I've almost laughed since I been out! Steve *Lennox?*

MARCIE: Yeah, well. At least he was around.

VICTOR: Ya got me there.

MARCIE: We have nothing to talk about.

VICTOR: Look, I'm a little…on edge. So I'm not gonna argue. I'm not gonna ask why you didn't visit, or send me anything but divorce forms. You had reasons. Alright. But we need to talk about visitation. I'm going to want to see our son.

MARCIE: Victor… *(Beat)* We don't have a son.

VICTOR: Where is he?

MARCIE: You need to understand what I just said.

VICTOR: Where is he?

MARCIE: My son is in school. Victor… I was seeing Steve…when you and I were married.

VICTOR: Do not…

MARCIE: He and I…

VICTOR: Do not play with me like this.

MARCIE: I don't know how else to say it.

VICTOR: My son…

MARCIE: He's not…

VICTOR: My son…

MARCIE: He's not your…

VICTOR: …is the only thing that's kept me *alive*! I got a *stack* of letters I wrote him. Didn't send them because you'd only throw them away. He's all I was living for…

MARCIE: I'm so sorry.

VICTOR: My son thinks about me. He thinks about me and…and…he…

MARCIE: He doesn't know you exist. Why would he? I made Steve…take a test, to be sure. *(Shows him the papers).* Here.

VICTOR: It's not true.

MARCIE: Really. I'm sorry.

VICTOR: Why would you do something like this? When we were married?

MARCIE: I hated myself. I felt so guilty. I still do. But I was younger. And I was alone *all* the *time.* You were always...you were always... *(Beat, then sadly as she readies to leave)* ...working.

(End of scene)

Scene 14

(In the library. BELLEVILLE *is looking through a book when* UNSWORTH *arrives, carrying a leather-covered volume. Both smile, though hers may be a bit sad.)*

UNSWORTH: Professor Belleville.

BELLEVILLE: Hello!

UNSWORTH: I've missed you in the cafeteria. I went by your office, they said you were still traveling.

BELLEVILLE: I had to stay an extra day. Did you get the books I left for you?

UNSWORTH: I did. I start every class with a story. It works wonderfully.

BELLEVILLE: How's the drooler?

UNSWORTH: Positively dry-mouthed!

BELLEVILLE: Terrific! A good story is magic.

UNSWORTH: It is.

*(*BELLEVILLE *and* UNSWORTH *both smile. Search for something to say. A moment of quiet. Then he shows her the book he's carrying)*

UNSWORTH: You also left *The Razor's Edge.*

BELLEVILLE: It's for you. Your students might like it too. When you get a chance you should read it.

UNSWORTH: I did.

BELLEVILLE: Already?

UNSWORTH: Last night. When I'm not out disco dancing I curl up with a book.

BELLEVILLE: 'Disco dancing'?

UNSWORTH: I was joking. I don't go out much, so it's even funnier when you're me. Do they still disco dance?

BELLEVILLE: I don't know. I don't go out much either. *(Again, a pause)* Did you like the book?

UNSWORTH: I did. He throws away a fortune.

BELLEVILLE: He does. But he gains so much.

UNSWORTH: Not the girl though.

BELLEVILLE: No. It's like real life that way. Not an entirely happy ending. Tolstoy once said that people who like happy endings are the same people who like pickled cabbage.

UNSWORTH: Did he really say that?

BELLEVILLE: God no. But when you're a literature prof and you say "Tolstoy said", people believe you. They'll never look it up.

UNSWORTH: I was inspired by the book. And I uh...I'd like you to um, to have dinner with me tonight. This is not like me. I'm taking a chance but...for a year you and I have talked and...I've always been really shy... but I think you like me. I really think you do. And I like you a lot, too. So we should do this. We should... do this.

BELLEVILLE: I...can't.

UNSWORTH: Oh...I didn't think you were seeing...

BELLEVILLE: I'm not. I wanted to keep it quiet until it was certain but...I was traveling to Claremont University...I got an offer...

UNSWORTH: All the way out in...?

BELLEVILLE: Yes. I have to take it. I'd love to stay here... but I can't afford to pass up the salary.

UNSWORTH: Oh.

BELLEVILLE: So…I think I'm going. I've got nothing here to…I mean, it's a great opportunity. There.

UNSWORTH: I'm sure. *(He looks away for a moment. Silence. Then he hands her the book)* Thank you…

BELLEVILLE: No. It's for you.

UNSWORTH: It…it looks expensive. I really shouldn't…

BELLEVILLE: It's not about the money.

(Both BELLEVILLE's *and* UNSWORTH's *hands are on the book, inches away from each other. They are both aware of this. Neither knows what to do. Neither moves. Lights down.)*

(End of scene)

Scene 15

*(*DON *in his office at the end of the day.* LETTY *enters and catches him off guard. She is straight-faced, unsmiling, all business.)*

DON: Hey. Why're you here?

LETTY: Where's the rest of your office?

DON: Let 'em go early. I was closing up. Have a seat.

LETTY: I don't think…

DON: *(Crossly)* I'm not takin' no for an answer. *(He smiles, goes friendly)* See? That's how you be forceful. I always liked you Letty, even if you smile alot. I sometimes check, see if my zipper's down. *(Beat)* That's a joke. *(Beat, sees no smile.)* I bet you laugh internally. *(Rolls his eyes a little when he sees she may be angry.)* O K: I was a jackass. I apologize. But good news: I can make the conference. *(Smiles even wider. Puts his hands up)* Don't thank me with words. Just reward me with scotch.

LETTY: What do you...?

DON: My brother. We haven't talked in years. I left a message for him. It was the hardest thing I could ever do. But I *did it!* He called me back. He'd love to watch Danny.

LETTY: I don't...

DON: He and my Frank kept in touch. He and Danny are great friends. Danny's excited, he really wants to stay with his uncle. I been thinking of my Frank, what he'd want me to do. Otherwise I wouldn't have called my brother in a *million* years.

LETTY: Don. You don't have to worry about the conference. We hired a certified consultant to go.

DON: See, your jokes stink. 'Cause I already know we can't afford that.

LETTY: *(She can't look at him. Emotionlessly)* You refused to go to the conference. I looked at your employment contract. That falls under insubordination. So we're hiring the consultant with the money we save from letting you go.

DON: Come on! Now you sound like your boss!

LETTY: She's approved it.

DON: No kiddin' she'd approve it! She's been trying for years to find an excuse to fire me, hire someone cheaper. Don't you have any sense? Can't you see how she played you?

LETTY: *(Trying to be tough, but something has broken in her.)* I...I didn't...

DON: Letty, I *told* you—I was trying to make this work. Why'd you go behind my back?

LETTY: I didn't think you'd change.

DON: I got a grandson to support. I...I busted my ass to be good to you.

LETTY: I'm sorry.

DON: All this, over some insurance conference?

LETTY: I can't afford to care anymore, Don.

DON: Now I know what my own son hated about me. Well, at least I found my soul. I hope you know what you're doing with yours.

(VICTOR *enters. He's preoccupied, carrying the weight of shame on his shoulders.* DON *starts to go over to meet him but* LETTY *stops* DON.)

LETTY: I'll get it, Don. You don't work here anymore. (*She steps over.*) I'm sorry. This office is closed.

VICTOR: I have to get a bond.

LETTY: Come back in the morning.

VICTOR: I need it so I can work tomorrow.

LETTY: For where?

(VICTOR *hands* LETTY *the paper. She hands a paper back and points to a section.*)

LETTY: Fill this.

VICTOR: (*Pointing to the paper*) Wait. That's more money than they said.

LETTY: There's state service tax.

VICTOR: (*Checks his pockets, pulls out some wrinkled bills*) I don't...I'm a little...I didn't know, the tax.

(LETTY *pulls the paper back.*)

VICTOR: Wait. (*He checks the rest of his pockets, finds he has no more money and makes a motion to her, palms open*) I don't...

LETTY: Could you leave please?

VICTOR: I need…I can go ask…

LETTY: The office is closed.

VICTOR: If I don't…could you…maybe…

LETTY: Come back tomorrow with the full fee or…

VICTOR: I can't! I need to *work* tomorrow.

LETTY: You need to go. *(She half looks over to* DON *for help, then decides to be tougher)*

VICTOR: If you could just… *(Trying to calm himself. Swallows)* give me a break here.

LETTY: If you don't go I'll call the police.

VICTOR: Don't *do* that. I need to…

LETTY: And you haven't got the *fee.*

VICTOR: Yeah, I can make all kinds of money, the things I can do! Is that what you're saying to me?!

*(*LETTY *picks up the phone.* VICTOR *slaps it out of her hand.)*

DON: Whoa buddy. Whoa.

VICTOR: You fucking…you can't even be human to me? This is the kind of world you wanna live in? You can't give me a *minute* of time…

*(*VICTOR *advances on* LETTY *in blind anger.* DON *sees this and moves forward)*

DON: Whoa pal! Hey!

LETTY: I'm calling the police!

VICTOR: *(In a fury)* This is how you want to live? Being like this to *me*? I'm begging to get a job cleaning up *shit* and you…!

*(*VICTOR *moves close to* LETTY. DON, *from behind him, grabs* VICTOR's *shoulder.* VICTOR, *threatened, reaches for a pair of scissors or a letter opener that is on the desk and*

blindly swings them around and into DON's *stomach.*
He stabs again, in a rage. DON *collapses to the floor with*
VICTOR *holding the bloody scissors.*)

VICTOR: *(Screaming)* I just need to get a job and you
do this to me?! You do this!? You fucking make me
do this?! *(He begins to cry but holds it back as he comes to
realize what he's done.)* Get up mister. Just get up. I'll
help you. I will. Come on. Get up. Get up.

(Lights down)

(End of scene)

Scene 16

*(*VICTOR *sits on the sofa. He's ripping papers, then dropping
them into a trash can. This goes on until* SIMON *enters and
stands a safe distance away.* VICTOR *looks up, still ripping
papers, and stares at* SIMON, *showing little surprise.)*

SIMON: Know who I am?

VICTOR: I think so.

SIMON: Who am I?

VICTOR: You were smaller, last time I saw you. In court.

SIMON: I'm bigger now. Thought I'd come see you. *(He
expects a reply, gets none.)* I was waiting outside. Saw
you hurrying to get back here. Why were you running?

*(*VICTOR *is still stunned and says nothing.)*

SIMON: What are you ripping?

VICTOR: Letters I wrote.

SIMON: Here. *(He takes bills from his pocket and tosses
them to the floor.)* There's some money.

*(*VICTOR *looks at it, doesn't move)*

SIMON: That's what you wanted, right? *(He takes the gun from his waistband and holds it at his side.)* Pick it up.

VICTOR: Why?

SIMON: Because that's what you wanted. So pick it. The fuck. Up.

VICTOR: Do crazy things when you're scared, huh? You don't act like yourself.

SIMON: Take the money!

VICTOR: No. *(He stands.)*

SIMON: Whattaya doing?

VICTOR: Seein' what you'll do.

SIMON: Sit down!

(VICTOR steps forward)

VICTOR: If you want to shoot, go ahead. Here, I'll make it easy. *(He takes the bloody scissors from his pocket. He steps forward again.)*

SIMON: I'm not kidding, man! *(He pulls back the hammer of the gun.)*

VICTOR: There's the door. You want to run, run. But if you want to shoot, shoot. *(Beat)* Go ahead. Be brave.

SIMON: SIT DOWN! YOU HEAR ME? SIT DOWN!

(VICTOR is six feet away. SIMON grasps the gun with two shaky hands and levels it between VICTOR's eyes. SIMON glances back at the door, then again to VICTOR.)

SIMON: STOP MOVING! STOP! FUCKING! *MOVING!!!*

(VICTOR swiftly raises the scissors above his head and charges forward. Blackout.)

(End of scene)

Scene 17

(SIMON *enters, physically drained.* JANSON *at her desk, surprised, then angry.*)

SIMON: Hey.

JANSON: You were scheduled for noon.

SIMON: I'm a little late.

JANSON: Noon yesterday. You know what happens if you don't call in.

SIMON: My file goes back to county. I go to jail. No exceptions.

JANSON: Where were you?

(*Pause, where he almost doesn't answer. Then he starts, quietly.*)

SIMON: I went to see that guy who took everything we had.
I pointed the gun at his face…
He started walking over…
My hand is sweating and shaking. And I want to be strong but…I can't be the person I want to be…So I closed my eyes. And I pulled the trigger anyway.
The safety was on.
I wasn't sure how to take it off, and I'm trying to fix it and I dropped the damn thing and…you won't believe it…we were both so scared, I guess. We started laughing. After a second, his laugh…wasn't like mine. He walked to the table and kicked over these candles. The sofa went up. Curtains. All burning. And this guy, he just *sits down.* I'm pulling him up: *Run! We gotta run!*
Minute earlier I tried to kill him but now I'm *screaming*: Run, man! *We gotta run!* But he kept punching and pulling away…
All the fire and smoke. I had to get out.

He stayed.

You get what you want, and it's not…

JANSON: Is that what you wanted?

SIMON: Maybe I was pretending.

JANSON: So who do you pretend to be now?

SIMON: I dunno. Maybe a stripper. *(Beat, then serious)* I don't care about my file. I don't care if I go to jail.

JANSON: Don't worry about the file. But let's tell someone what happened. I know a guy at the police station. He'll understand. *(Motions to the door)*

SIMON: O K.

JANSON: On the way…we can drive by the old store. See it in the daylight.

SIMON: You sure?

JANSON: Yeah.

SIMON: Then what?

JANSON: I'll buy you a beer.

SIMON: You serious?

JANSON: God, you *are* young and dumb.

SIMON: *(About to protest, but then calms, realizes the truth)* I…! I can't help it.

JANSON: I know. I don't care.

(JANSON and SIMON walk out and close the door. Lights down)

(End of scene)

Scene 18

(MARIE's *office.* LETTY *enters without knocking. Both are in dark dress.*)

MARIE: Hey. You're late. It's O K. I was worried. Were you at the doctor?

LETTY: I went yesterday. Everything's fine.

MARIE: Good.

LETTY: Yeah. That's good. I was here early. In Spence's office. Talking with him.

MARIE: About what?

LETTY: I told him I lied about sick leave. Told him about the problems with the conference. Know what he said? "Why doesn't Marie just go?" You're still certified.

MARIE: So.

LETTY: Why did you lie?

MARIE: You must have misunderstood. I have seniority—it's not my job to go. I ordered you. It was to make you tougher, to have you figure it out. I couldn't have known this would happen. I'm sorry.

LETTY: Your apology means nothing.

MARIE: Let's not talk about this now.

LETTY: When should we talk about it? After we bury Don today?

MARIE: Watch yourself. I'm sure you're on thin ice with Spence.

LETTY: He's less happy with you—that you knew I abused sick leave but kept it from him. That violates policy too. I told him I was thinking about a lawsuit…

MARIE: Oh come on!

LETTY: ...over the stress. Over unsafe conditions at Don's office. I showed him my own contract—I'm within my rights. He's worried about our reputation. He convinced me not file a suit.

MARIE: What? He offered you Don's office? Good. Go to that backwater.

LETTY: No. He offered me yours. You're going to Don's.

MARIE: Yeah right. I'm overqualified for....

LETTY: You should clean out your desk.

MARIE: You can't be serious!

LETTY: He wants to see you now.

MARIE: This is insane. It's not true.

LETTY: He's waiting.

MARIE: If I go in there I'll have your job in two minutes.

LETTY: Then go.

(A moment, where LETTY *and* MARIE *wait to see who has the upper hand.)*

MARIE: *(She won't say it, but she's asking for mercy.)* Letty. Come on. I don't want to get wrapped up in some fight. Let's...

LETTY: I spent two nights at home, crying and crying. Then I stopped. From now on, I don't take shit off anyone.

MARIE: That's what I taught you! So listen to me!

LETTY: *(With deep malice. Teeth clenched. Motions to the door)* No. *(Beat)* Now hurry up. I hate "time theft".

(End of scene)

Scene 19

(BELLEVILLE *knocks on the front door of a small house.*
UNSWORTH *opens, wearing comfortable clothes—the first
time he doesn't have on a tie.*)

UNSWORTH: Gosh. Hi.

BELLEVILLE: Hi. How are you?

UNSWORTH: O K, I guess.

BELLEVILLE: I didn't see you for a week. I thought you
might be mad. So I stopped by your office. I didn't
know. I was so sorry to hear…

UNSWORTH: It's been a heck of a time. I should have
called you, but…

BELLEVILLE: Oh, don't apologize…

UNSWORTH: I thought about you a lot.

BELLEVILLE: I thought about you too. So much.

UNSWORTH: Did you sign on for Claremont yet?

BELLEVILLE: No. I was supposed to fly out tonight. I
told them to wait. I had to see you, when I heard. But
why are you worrying about me?

UNSWORTH: Keeps my mind off other things.

BELLEVILLE: What exactly happened?

UNSWORTH: My brother. He was in an altercation. At
his office. He was killed.

BELLEVILLE: I'm so…

UNSWORTH: An argument. Started over money. I've
spent the week thinking of him. And looking at myself,
too. All these years, just doing my job. Even though I
was a terrible teacher.

BELLEVILLE: You're not…

UNSWORTH: I am. My students never took to me.

BELLEVILLE: They're idiots. That's why they're in college.

UNSWORTH: Funny thing is, I never liked business or finance. Believe it or not...I had my heart set on literature.

BELLEVILLE: Then why didn't you study it?

UNSWORTH: My father was a businessman. A tough one, in and out of the office. He'd yell "I spent good money on your shoes, don't scuff them!" or "You better get straight As, after what I paid for your tuition!" He'd talk about the price of the food we were eating or the car we drove. He scared us, screaming how hard he worked for his money.
(Beat)
My brother. Don. He was a wonderful child, always studying. He'd go to the library, down the street. When it was nice out, he'd sit in a park with his schoolbooks and read.
(Beat)
One day he was in that park and a...a man sat next to him. My brother, he was eleven and this...this creep he...he touched him and...
When Donny came home he cried for hours. My father called the police. We were all in the living room together, because he was frightened to be alone. And the officer said:
"Did the man have a knife or did he threaten you?" Donny shook his head no and the officer said: "So he sat next to you, and at first you stood up, right?" And my brother nodded. And then the officer asked, "Why didn't you run away?"
And my crying eleven year-old brother said: "That man took my book bag and wouldn't give it back. Daddy made me promise never to come home without my books. He said they cost him so much money."

(He almost stops, but knows he must go on.)
My father never mentioned money again. But he spent
a lot of it. On liquor. 'Til a couple months later he tried
to drive home, blind drunk.
(Beat)
He was smart about finance, though. Had excellent life
insurance. It paid my way through college. Provided I
studied business.
Don and I were never the same. He grew colder. We
drifted apart.
(Beat)
My brother had a grandson. I'm adopting him. He's
learned how cruel the world can be. I think I can teach
him…it can have beauty too. I can teach him that.

BELLEVILLE: Maybe you need someone to help you?

UNSWORTH: No. I'm taking a leave and… *(Suddenly
realizes her offer)* Oh, oh yes! I could! But I thought you
were…?

BELLEVILLE: I'm not sure.

UNSWORTH: If you stayed…it would be a big risk.

BELLEVILLE: I know. But why else are we alive, if not to
take these great and mad chances? Tolstoy said that.

UNSWORTH: Did he?

BELLEVILLE: Look it up. *(Nods toward the door)* Can I
come in?

UNSWORTH: Sure. His name is Danny. He's so… When
you meet him, I know you'll fall in love.

BELLEVILLE: Let's go.

*(UNSWORTH reaches out and offers his hand. BELLEVILLE
takes it. They go in.)*

END OF PLAY